Am I Right...eous

Am I Right...eous

(Understanding Righteousness)

Tommie Brown

Xulon Press

Xulon Press
2301 Lucien Way #415
Maitland, FL 32751
407.339.4217
www.xulonpress.com

Unless otherwise indicated, SScripture quotations taken from the King James Version (KJV) – *public domain.*

Scripture quotations taken from the Holy Bible, New International Version (NIV). Copyright © 1973, 1978, 1984, 2011 by Biblica, Inc.™. Used by permission. All rights reserved.

Scripture quotations taken from the Gods Word Translation (GW) copyright ©1995 by Baker Publishing Group.

Scripture quotations taken from the Amplified Bible (AMP). Copyright © 1954, 1958, 1962, 1964, 1965, 1987 by The Lockman Foundation. Used by permission. All rights reserved.

Scripture quotations taken from the Holy Bible, New Living Translation (NLT). Copyright ©1996, 2004, 2007 by Tyndale House Foundation. Used by permission of Tyndale House Publishers, Inc.

Scripture quotations taken from the English Standard Version (ESV). Copyright © 2001 by Crossway, a publishing ministry of Good News Publishers. Used by permission. All rights reserved.

Scripture quotations taken from the New King James Version (NKJV). Copyright © 1982 by Thomas Nelson, Inc. Used by permission. All rights reserved.

Scripture quotations taken from the Holy Bible, New International Version (NIV). Copyright © 1973, 1978, 1984, 2011 by Biblica, Inc.™. Used by permission. All rights reserved.

Printed in the United States of America.

ISBN-13: 978-1-6322-1062-3

AM I Right...eous?

"I have proclaimed the good news of righteousness in the great assembly, I did not restrain my lips, O Lord, You yourself know; I have not hidden your Righteousness within my heart, I have declared your faithfulness and your salvation, I have not concealed your lovingkindness and your truth from the great assembly."

Is 40:9,10

Table of Contents

Chapter 1

———◦◉◦———

Understanding Righteousness

Some years ago, I was talking on the phone to a close friend, a man I'd known for many years. During our conversation, he made a comment which I believe is one of the greatest hindrances to people receiving all that God has in store for them.

After giving a great deal of thought to our conversation, and after having spent time searching the scriptures and listening to my heart, I decided to write this book in hope that it might bring some light to everyone who might feel or think the way my friend did when he made the comment.

I'll begin at the beginning!

Several years ago, I was discussing with my friend, how God had blessed my wife and me with favor in so many ways during the building of our home. I told him about how accommodating the bank had been, and how the insurance agent had worked really hard to get us a good rate, etc...

After I'd finished speaking He said,"God is really on your side! He's really looking out for you!" "He really cares about you!" I replied, " He cares about all of His children. Then he said, "But you're special so He's really looking out for you!"

To be perfectly honest with you, at first I thought it was pretty neat that he would think that God would consider me special and I basked in it for a moment. But the more I thought about the comment, the more I saw that what he was saying was that I'd somehow earned the right to be considered special by God because of something I'd done and he, because of some things he had done or had not done, had not earned that right.

I'd had the privilege of working with this individual for several years and during that time I came to know him as a man of honor, integrity and courage. He never buckled under the pressure of politics or compromised his convictions. He wasn't a perfect man, like so many of us, he made mistakes and some wrong decisions but, he was a good man.

In the year 2000, the Lord began to deal with my heart about ministry. In 2001 I resigned from the police department and moved to Oklahoma to attend Rhema Bible Training Center. In 2003, I graduated and moved back to Jackson, where I have since served in several capacities of ministry. This is what my friend was referring to when he said I was one of God's favorites. He was saying it was because of the decision I'd made to pursue ministry that I was special in God's eyes.

I learned long before I went away to ministry school, that we can do nothing to earn the favor of God. The favor of God is a gift from God to all who will receive it by receiving Jesus Christ as their personal Lord and Savior. Ephesians 2:8,9 reads, *"For by grace are you saved through faith, and that not of yourselves, it is a gift of God, not of works, lest any man should boast."*

I remember sometime ago, when I was sitting and thinking about having obeyed God by answering the call to go into full time ministry. I was pleased with the decision and was thinking to myself, God must really be pleased with me; He must really love me because I have obeyed Him. This was long before the conversation with my friend. I remember the Lord speaking to my heart and saying, "I loved you just as much before you accepted the call into ministry, as I do now that you have."

John 3:16 says, (this is Jesus himself speaking), "*For God so loved the world, that He gave His only begotten Son, that whosoever believeth on Him, should not perish but have everlasting life*". Jesus did not say, "For God so loved only those who make good decisions..."

Then in Romans 5:8 the Bible says,"But God shows and clearly proves His own love for us by the fact that while we were still sinners, Christ (the Messiah, the Anointed One) died for us.

> I John 4:10 NIV "*This is love: not that we loved God but that he loves us (All of us) and sent his Son as an atoning sacrifice for our sins.*"

Sometime back in the late 90's while I was attending, what was then called Layman's Bible School, at the church where I was a member, one of the classes I took was on the subject of Righteousness. The class literally changed my life! When I came to understand what it meant to be righteous, it ignited a hunger in me and set me on a path to grow up spiritually. I realized at that point that I had been stuck in a rut, spiritually speaking. I had managed to get inside the kingdom of God or inside the family of God; I was inside the door, but that was as far as I had been able to go because, like so many others, I struggled with the issues of not feeling worthy or good enough to be used by God. Whenever I would sin, I would spend the next six weeks to six months trying to work my way back into God's grace, because I didn't know any better. I just knew God didn't quickly forgive me! I thought he eventually would, but only after I did enough right things, said enough right things, prayed long enough or cried hard enough. The problem was this; the harder I worked to get God's approval, the more I seemed to fall back into sin and the more conscious of sin I became. Oftentimes I would just give up for months at a time. Then, eventually I would accept God's forgiveness and start all over again. This was a cycle for my life before I learned the truth according to God's Word.

Finally, one day the light came on for me; I realized; "I AM NOT A SINNER saved by grace, I WAS A SINNER who WAS SAVED by grace the moment I accepted Jesus Christ as my Lord and Savior. In other words, I was saved by grace SO I am no longer a sinner! You will get a better understanding of what I mean as I talk about Righteousness.

I WAS A SINNER - NOW **I AM** SAVED

I WAS AN UNBELIEVER - NOW **I AM** A BELIEVER

I WAS LOST - NOW **I AM** FOUND

I **WAS** IN THE KINGDOM OF DARKNESS - **I AM** IN THE KINGDOM OF GOD'S DEAR SON, THE KINGDOM OF LIGHT

I **WAS** SPIRITUALLY DEAD - NOW **I AM** ALIVE IN CHRIST JESUS!

Upon studying the subject of Righteousness, I realized that I had not fully understood what happened when I accepted Jesus Christ into my heart by inviting Him to become my Lord and Savior. II Corinthians 5:21 reads, *"For He (God the Father) has made him (Jesus) to be sin for us who knew no sin **that we might be made the righteousness of God in Him**.*

My problem was that I was trying hard to become righteous which led to my becoming more conscious of my sins. This sin consciousness had stunted my spiritual growth. But as I meditated on this scripture, I discovered the truth. This truth broke the chains that had before held me bound.

God in His great love for me, made Christ (Who himself was sinless) to become sin for me that I might become righteous - IN HIM. IN other words, He took my sin and gave me His righteousness. Another way to say it is; He took my sins, making me right with Him or putting me into right standing with Him and with The Father God.

When Jesus became my Savior, He became my righteousness, and through him I became the righteousness of God the Father because HE MADE me righteous IN Christ JESUS!

> I Corinthians 1:30 says, *But of Him (God) you are in Christ Jesus who of God (The Father) has been made unto us wisdom and righteousness and sanctification and redemption. (Christ has been made unto us Righteousness).*

So then, my problem was that I was trying to do something I could never do. That is, to become righteous on my own. The good news is that Christ already did it. He'd already made me righteous without my help. My job was to simply receive, by becoming more righteousness- conscious, what Christ had already done. I could only do that by searching the scriptures to find out what Christ did for us when He died, was buried, rose again and ascended into heaven and sat down at the right hand of the Father.

For the past couple of paragraphs, I've been talking about righteousness. I get excited all over again every time I hear or see the word. I remember the first time I heard the definition of Righteousness. It means, to be in right standing with God. To be in right standing with God means the ability to stand in the presence of God without the sense of guilt or inferiority; it means the ability to stand in the presence of God as though you never sinned.

The more righteousness conscious I became, the less sin conscious I became. I finally accepted the fact that Jesus took my sin and gave me His righteousness, giving me the liberty to receive all that Christ did for me at Calvary as a part of the Father's plan of redemption. Jesus went through a lot to redeem me! He was beaten beyond recognition; He was mocked, spat on, stabbed and crucified. He shed his blood, went to hell, fought with Satan and the host of darkness and won the victory just for me. On the third day he rose for me. He ascended into heaven and sat down at the right hand of the throne of God for me and for all who believe in Him. He did all this to make me righteous. So, the least I could do was receive it!

The truth of the matter is this: I could NEVER under any circumstance, or in any way make myself righteous. I could not earn it by doing good deeds or buy it with all the money in the world; I could not manufacture it; I could not duplicate it, etc. The only thing I could do was to receive it as a gift which was purchased with the precious blood of Jesus. And there is only one name through which I can receive it. It is the Name of the one whose blood was shed, it is the Name, Jesus Christ.

Let me share with you now what the Scriptures have to say about the Name of Jesus! In the book of Acts chapter 4:8 it reads, *"Then Peter, filled with the Holy Spirit, said to them: "Rulers and elders of the people! 9 If we are being called to account today for an act of kindness shown to a man who was lame and are being asked how he was healed, 10 then know this, you and all the people of Israel: It is by the Name of Jesus Christ of Nazareth whom you crucified but who God raised from the dead, that this man stands before you healed. 11 Jesus is "'the stone you builders rejected which has become the cornerstone.' 12 Salvation is found in no one else, for there is no other name under heaven given to mankind by which we must be saved."*

This word saved comes from the greek word "sozo" and it means to save, to deliver, to protect, heal, to preserve, to do well, to make whole. In essence, it means the following:

1) to save, keep safe and sound, to rescue from danger or destruction

2) To rescue one from peril

3) To save a suffering one from perishing; one suffering from disease, to make well, heal, restore to health

4) To deliver from penalties of judgement

5) To save from the evils which obstruct the reception of deliverance

Salvation from all these things listed above is available to those who will believe on and call on the Name of Jesus in faith! And this salvation is a gift from our Father God! Ephesians 2:8,9 says, "*For by grace are we SAVED through faith and that not of ourselves, it is a gift of God, not of works lest any man should boast*!

Salvation is a gift! Righteousness is a gift! Sanctification is a gift! Redemption is a gift! Righteousness is a free gift to us from our Father God.

It is not free because it comes without a price. In fact it had the greatest price placed upon it that has ever been placed upon anything of value at any time in human history! The price was Jesus' own blood, and he paid it ALL! Thank God HE PAID IT ALL! Now we get to enjoy the benefit of being in right standing with God our father and can fully expect Him to hear our prayers and answer them!

Because it is a free gift, it puts all men on the same plane to obtain it. The rich man can't buy it, otherwise he would buy it all and sell it to others for a profit. The strong man can't take it, otherwise he would hoard it all for himself and for the few people with whom he cares to share it. The wise man can't figure it out because it is far too simple for him. He is confused by the whole idea that righteousness could come by simply having faith in what Jesus Christ did on our behalf on Calvary over 2000 years ago, and what He is doing on our behalf today as He is seated at the right hand of the Father. It makes no sense at all to the wise man who has only earthly wisdom, how Jesus Christ and The Father God can live in our hearts in the person of the Holy Spirit. (I Kings 8:27 and I Corinthians 3:16)

In I Corinthians 1:17, the Apostle Paul says by the inspiration of the Holy Spirit, *"For Christ sent me not to baptize but to preach the gospel not with wisdom of words lest the cross of Christ should be made of non effect. 18 For the preaching of the cross is to them that perish foolishness but unto us which are saved, it is the power of God. 19 For it is written, I will destroy the wisdom of the wise and the understanding of the prudent (and ignore the best ideas of man, even the most brilliant of them). I will destroy all human plans of salvation no matter how wise they seem to be 20.. Has not God made the wisdom of this world look foolish? 21 For since in accordance with the wisdom of God the world had never in reality, by means of its wisdom come to know God, it was God's good pleasure to save people who put their faith in Him. 25 This so-called foolish plan of God (foolish according to the wisdom of men) is far wiser than the wisest plan of the wisest man. And what seems feeble in God is stronger than the strongest of men.*

V26 For see your calling brethren, how not many wise men after the flesh, not many mighty, not many noble are called. 27 But God has chosen the foolish things of the world to confound the wise, and God has chosen the weak things of the world to confound the things that are mighty. 28 And the base things of the world and the things which are despised has God chosen, yea and the things which are not to bring to nought things which are. 29 that no man should glory in his presence

Chapter 2

———◦◉◦———

Growing Up Spiritually

The number one reason why the believer must understand righteousness and become righteousness conscious is so that he can move on from the place of spiritual infancy or babyhood to spiritual maturity so that he/she can be fruitful and multiply. You see, God's plan is to use every believer in some aspect of ministry for the advancement of the kingdom of God.

Spiritual babies are needy, selfish, irresponsible and require a lot of attention and maintenance. They have to be pampered, spoon fed, they are selfish, and they bear no fruit. They are primarily dependent upon others for practically everything. Spiritual adults on the other hand, are responsible, low maintenance, confident, unselfish and totally dependent upon God and skilled in fruit bearing.

Chronological age has little to do with spiritual maturity. This also holds true regarding academic education, financial status, social status and even the number of years one has been a believer. A person could have been in the church for forty years and still be a spiritual baby. Spiritual maturity does not come with church attendance, but as a result of one being hungry and thirsty for God and satisfying that hunger and thirst with a relentless pursuit of the Word of God through reading, studying, meditating and acting upon it.

God can take a man who has little or no formal education, one who's public speaking ability has much to be desired; one who is frail in statue or who has had a rough, colorful or colorless past; and use him mightily when he's willing to yield himself to the Word and will of God! Oftentimes, not always, men who are rich or strong in their own rite find it hard to yield to God because of the confidence they've built in themselves or the systems that have helped them achieve their status. However, those who will truly accept Jesus Christ as their Savior and Lord and truly submit themselves to His word and His Spirit, the Holy Spirit guides them into the truth. Those who cooperate with the Holy Spirit go on to become great men/women of God.

The Apostle Paul helped me out a lot when he spoke to the believers at Corinth in his letter to them about how God had called and chosen them in spite of the absence of the qualities that would have been required had they been chosen by men instead of by God, to do the work of the ministry. God has a different standard or different measuring stick that he uses to choose men. He doesn't look at the outward appearance but at the heart. He doesn't look at what you have but what you're willing to give; he doesn't care so much about what you know, as much as he does about what you're willing to learn. He doesn't look at how strong you are but how strong you're willing to become. He doesn't look at how independent you are, but how dependent upon him you're willing to become.

I want to look at I Corinthians 1:26 again, this time from a different translation;

> *"My brothers think what sort of people you are whom God has called. Not many of you were wise according to worldly standards, not many in positions of power, not many born of noble parents, but God has chosen what the world calls foolish to shame the wise, and God has chosen what the world calls weak to shame the strong and God has chosen what the world counts poor and insignificant and things that are to it, unreal, to nullify its realities so in His presence no human being might have anything to boast of.*

If God had called and chosen only those men who were wise (by the world's standard) strong or rich, I would never have made the cut, neither would many of the people He used in His work throughout the church age or the pre-church age for that matter. Only Jesus was perfect. But God chose ordinary men, and through them He did extraordinary things. He chose fisherman, a tax collector, a physician and the likes to turn the world upside down. He even used a man whose former occupation was persecuting Christians. God gave him the revelation of the mysteries of His plan of redemption which had been hidden throughout the ages, then inspired Him to write two-thirds of the New Testament.

If God could use a man like that, He can surely use me and you! Thank the Lord!!

This man to whom I'm referring is the Apostle Paul. Paul was the most influential apostle of the New Testament. As I stated before, he was used mightily by God in making known God's plan of redemption and God's unsearchable riches which He has given us in Christ Jesus.

How in the world was God able to use a man who had persecuted the Church of the Lord Jesus Christ by having Christians beaten, imprisoned and even consenting to their deaths? In fact what Paul was doing in all actuality was persecuting Christ himself, because the Church is Christ's body. That is why Jesus asked Paul (then Saul) the question in Acts 9:4 *"Saul, Saul, why do you persecute me?"* How in the world would or could Jesus use someone who had such a past? Something must have taken place in Paul's life that changed him. What could possibly have taken place in his life that it would change him from a man who persecuted the church into a man who made a greater contribution to the establishment, growth and development of the church than anyone other than Jesus Christ himself, because of his commitment to Christ and the Gospel?

This is what took place in Paul's life that forever changed him: Paul received from Christ, the revelation of righteousness! He expressed that revelation in Galatians 3:20 when he says, "I am crucified with Christ, nevertheless I live, yet not I but Christ liveth in me: and the life which I now live in the flesh, I live by the faith of the Son of God who loved me and gave himself for me." He goes on to say in verse 21 *"I do not nullify the grace of God for if righteousness comes by the law then Christ died in vain." Paul is saying that this righteousness is not the result of my good works or my own effort, but by the grace of God through faith, otherwise Christ might as well have not died.*

When a man receives Jesus Christ as his personal Lord and Savior, he becomes a brand new man, a new person altogether. Paul puts it this way in II Corinthians 5:17,

"Therefore if any man be in Christ he is a new creature (creation), old things are passed away, behold all things are become new". When a man receives Christ as his personal Lord and Savior, he becomes a new creation, a man who never before existed.

The apostle Paul could have spent the rest of his life after his conversion living under condemnation for the unspeakable sin of persecuting Christians, but he didn't. He understood that once he received Jesus Christ as His Savior and Lord, at that very moment God forgave him! Let me ask you a question; Are your sins greater than Paul's? Have you committed any sin that would be considered greater than persecuting Christians, having them imprisoned, having them beaten and put to death, or according to Jesus, having persecuted Jesus Christ Himself by doing such? When Jesus died on the cross, He died for our sins, past present and future. He died for Paul's sins even though Paul had not yet committed them. On the day when Paul, or Saul (his name before his conversion) was on his way to Damascus to persecute more of Christ followers, Jesus appeared to him and revealed Himself to him as the Messiah, the one whom Saul was persecuting. At that moment, Paul accepted Jesus as his Savior and Lord. Jesus forgave Paul for all the awful things he had done and called him into ministry. From that time on, Paul lived his life as one who understood and accepted his right standing with God; Christ had become his Righteousness!

Jesus died for our sins, past present and future. Does that mean we can just live a life of sin; sinning at will without any consequences? Absolutely not!

Let's take a look at what the apostle John has to say in his letter to the church; John 1:8 *"If we say we have no sin, we deceive ourselves and the truth is not in us. 9 If we confess our sins, He is faithful and just to forgive our sins and to cleanse us from all unrighteousness. 10 If we say that we have not sinned, we make him a liar and his word is not in us. I John 2:1 My little children, these things I write unto you that you sin not (that you keep clear of sin), But if anyone should sin we have one who can plead for us with the Father, Jesus Christ, the Righteous.*

Sin without repentance brings about judgement. Sinning without a repentant heart results in a seared conscience which leads to willful and habitual sin. Willful sin left unchecked leads to spiritual death and even physical death. But, this is the good news, If we confess our sins to God and repent of them, He is faithful and just to forgive us and to cleanse us from all unrighteousness, making us righteous or restoring us to right standing with Him!

Chapter 3

————◦◉◦————

The Sin-free Life

For many years, like so many other Christians, I did not fully understand what it meant to live a sin-free life. I was led to believe, by people who obviously knew as little as I did on the subject of Righteousness, that a Christian eventually reaches a level of maturity where he/she is no longer tempted by sin. I later learned that it was the farthest thing from the truth. What is true is that a Christian can reach a level of spiritual maturity where he no longer gives in to the temptation to sin. The temptation comes, but he resist's it, he gives no place to it.

Most Christians and many non-Christians have heard the story about Jesus being tempted in the wilderness by the devil. Let's take a look at what happened in the Gospel of Luke beginning in chapter 4:1 kjv. *And Jesus being full of the Holy Ghost returned from Jordan and*

21

was led by the Spirit into the wilderness 2 being tempted forty days by the devil. And in those days he ate nothing, and afterwards when they had ended, He was hungry. 3 And the devil said unto him. If you are the Son of God, command this stone to be made bread. 4 And Jesus answered him saying, It is written, "Man shall not live by bread alone but by every word of God. 5 And the devil, taking him up into a high mountain, showed him all the kingdoms of the world in a moments time 6 And the devil said unto him, All this power will I give thee, and the glory of them, for that is delivered unto me and to whomsoever I give it. 7 If thou therefore will worship me, all shall be thine. 8 And Jesus answered and said unto him, "Get thee behind me Satan for it is written, "Thou shalt worship the Lord your God and Him only shall thou serve. 9 And he brought him into Jerusalem and set him upon a pinnacle of the temple and said unto him "If thou be the Son of God, cast thyself down from hence, 10 for it is written, "He shall give his angels charge over thee: 11 and their hands shall bear thee up lest at anytime thou dash thy foot against a stone. 12 And Jesus answering said unto him, "It is said thou shall not tempt the Lord your God 13 And when the devil had ended all the temptations, he departed from him for a season. (Note, he left Jesus for a season, that was not the end of the devils attempts to tempt Jesus)

Jesus is our example. He was tempted but he resisted the devil. How did Jesus resist? He resisted with the written Word of God. How do we resist? We resist with the written Word of God! This is the only way we can resist temptation.

Most people overlook verse 13. It says *"And when the devil had ended ALL the temptation*; the Knox Translation says, *"when he had finished tempting him in every way"* ; the Modern Translation puts it this way, *"so after exhausting on him every kind of temptation*; *...he departed from him for a season, or 'till a fresh occasion should present itself.*

The devil tempted Jesus with every type of temptation while He was in the wilderness. Jesus did not give into the temptation but resisted every temptation with the written Word of God. The devil left Jesus at that time, but didn't give up. Jesus is our example, but He is more than that! He is the perfect person to represent us before our Father God, because He has personally experienced being tempted by the same devil we are tempted by. He took upon Himself an earthly body. He is the Word of God who became flesh and dwelt among us according to the Gospel of St. John chapter 1:1-5:

> *1 In the beginning was the Word, and the Word was with God, and the Word was God. 2 He was with God in the beginning. 3 Through him all things were made; without him nothing was made that has been made. 4 In him was life,*

and that life was the light of all mankind. 5 The light shines in the darkness, and the darkness has not overcome it.

In order to fully embrace the example Jesus set for us regarding resisting the temptation to sin, it is important that one fully grasp the understanding of who Jesus is as noted in the preceding scripture. These scriptures speak of the divinity and incarnation of Jesus Christ. In these scriptures, it is impossible not to see Jesus's connection to His Word! The Bible tells us that Jesus was the Word made flesh who dwelt among us; Jesus was the Word in the beginning; Jesus was the Word and was with God; Jesus was the Word who was God; Jesus was the Word who was with God in the beginning! Through the Word all things were made; without the Word, nothing was made that has been made; In the Word was life, and that life was the light of all mankind. The Word's light shines in the darkness, and the darkness has not overcome the Word's light...

When we come to understand these scriptures, we also come to understand the power of the spoken Word of God in resisting the tempter, Satan. I John 1:5 says, *"This then is the message which we have heard of him (Jesus), and declare unto you, that God is light and in Him there is no darkness at all."* We just read in St John's Gospel 1:5, In the Word was life, and the Word's life was the light of all mankind. The Word's light shines in darkness, and the darkness cannot overcome it (the light of the Word).

When Satan attempted to tempt Jesus, each time Jesus responded to the temptation by speaking the written Word of God until his resistance against the tempter caused him (Satan) to flee, at least for a season. When we speak the written Word of God in faith, we bring the very life of God onto the scene. His life is light and this light drives out the evil works of darkness!

Years ago when I worked with the police department, many business owners in high crime areas would install flood lights with motion sensors on the perimeter so that when someone attempted to come onto the property, the flood lights would illuminate them and in most cases the would-be thieves would run off or flee. The enemy works primarily under the cover of darkness or concealment. When light comes, darkness and the workers of darkness flee.

Jesus resisted the devil with the written Word of God. Jesus knows what it's like to be tempted and He knows what it takes to resist the devil. This makes Him both a perfect example to follow and a perfect Advocate for before the Father. The word Advocate means both intercessor and legal assistant. Hebrews 4:14 says, "Seeing that we have a great High Priest that is passed into the heavens, Jesus the Son of God, let us hold fast to our profession. 15 For we have not a high priest which cannot be touched with the feeling of our infirmities, but was in all points tempted like as we are, yet without sin." 16 Let us therefore come boldly unto the throne of grace that we may obtain mercy and find grace to help in the time of need.

When you speak the Word of God in answer to temptation, you speak from the very throne room of God. God backs His Word and the devil has to back down, hallelujah!!

Temptation comes in many forms. There is the temptation to eat unhealthy foods; the temptation to walk outside of love with people; the temptation to cheat on your spouse; the temptation to cheat on your taxes; the temptation to look at pornography; the temptation not to tithe; the temptation to look at movies you don't need to see; the temptation not to pay child support, not to pay your bills, not to go to church and an array of other things like the temptation not to read your Bible and pray..... and the list goes on! However, whatever the temptation, it can be overcome with the Word of God, if the one who is confronted with the temptation will use God's Word against it. Speaking the Word of God in faith when we are confronted with temptation, brings God onto the scene. The key to speaking the Gods Word in faith is reading your Bible and meditating on the scriptures until they come alive in your heart. Proverbs 4:20-22 "My son attend unto my words, incline your ear unto my sayings, let them not depart from your eyes, keep them in the midst of your heart, for they are life to all that find them and health unto all of their flesh

Joshua 1:8 - *This book of the law shall not depart out of thy mouth, but thou shalt meditate therein day and night and observe to do according to all that is written therein, for then thou shalt make thy way prosperous, and then thou shalt have good success.*

Chapter 4

---◈---

God Is Not The Tempter, Satan is!

In order that we might live in victory over temptation, there are several things we need establish in our hearts regarding God's role in our lives:

1. God is not the Tempter (James 1:13,14)

2. God will not allow you to be tempted above that which you are able if you will call upon Him. (Ps 145:18)

3. God will alway provide a way of escape (I Corinthians 10:13)

4. The temptation you're facing is not different from temptations others have faced. Others

5. have faced similar trials and have overcome
   them. (I Corinthians 10:13)

I really want to emphasize **Point #1** for this reason:

You can never have faith in someone or come to trust someone you feel is out to get you! You will never come to love someone who you think is trying to hurt you, even if you think they are trying to teach you a positive lesson.

I have a question for you. Would you go to a doctor for any type of procedure when you know he/she is known for operating on patients without first giving them anesthesia or, one that prescribes medicines to make their patients sicker in order to teach them a lesson? Of course not!

Many people, and even preachers, are misled to believe that it is God who's behind the temptations, tests and trials, and accounts it to his efforts to teach us a lesson. The danger of this type of thinking is that people will not resist something they feel God is doing to them.

They will attempt to endure the temptation and even testify to others that God is responsible for the trial or misfortune and unfortunately many times it is to their detriment.

Many people go to their graves believing this way. At their funerals you will hear it said by people who have no true understanding of God as a loving Father, that God took them because he needed one more flower! God doesn't need another flower, if He did, He would just speak it into existence! There is something Jesus said in the gospel of John chapter 10:10 that resonate with me each time I hear someone attempt to put the blame on God for their temptation, test or trial, and especially for the death of a loved one: Jesus said, "The thief comes but for to steal, kill and destroy, I came that you might have life and have it more abundantly".

And then in John 14:9 Jesus also said, *"...if you've seen me you've seen the Father"*. I can't speak for anyone else, but to me, Jesus is saying this; anything that is responsible for stealing from, killing or destroying man-kind, comes from the thief, Satan, or from the actions of men who either actively or passively give place to Satan in their lives through sin and unbelief. Anything that brings, adds, gives, improves or enhances life is from Jesus and from the Father! So, to say that God is "a" or "the" Tempter would be putting Him in the same category with Satan who is called the Tempter in the scriptures. (see Mat. 4:3). Death itself is the result of sin. Satan introduced sin into the earth when he approached Adam and Eve in the garden. Instead of resisting him by obeying God's command, they gave place to the devil by giving into his temptation to disobey God. When they disobeyed God, sin entered into the world and death resulted. From that point; because of Adam's sin, death became a reality for all of mankind. This means that every person that is born into this world is born into sin because of Adam's disobedience. Therefore every person has the need to be saved regardless of what he has done or has not done in his life. It was not God's intention for man to die, ever! The scripture that supports this can be found in Romans 5:12 Wherefore as by one man sin entered into the world and death by sin and so death passed upon all men, for that all have sinned.

Satan's plan was to forever separate man from God. His plan was to destroy the sweet fellowship man enjoyed with God in which God talked with him face to face. This is still Satan's plan, to steal, kill and destroy man. That is why Jesus told us that Satan comes to steal, kill and destroy. But God has a different plan for us. He sent Jesus to restore our fellowship with Him by restoring our standing with him as his sons and daughters. It was only by the precious blood of Jesus Christ His Son that this was made possible. For without the shedding of blood, there is no remission of sin. Jesus' blood washed our sins away, now we can stand in His presence as though we never sinned.

This is the life that Jesus spoke of; this is the life he came to give us. He came to give life, not to take it away; not to make life difficult, not steal our loved ones; not to put sickness upon us; not to send hurricanes and fires and violence in order to teach us a lesson!!!! You couldn't trust a God who would do those things to you, not even if you said you could. God is the giver of life! Now when our loved ones who are saved die, or when they are have not reached the age of accountability, God does **receive** them into heaven. God is not the Tempter, Satan is.

Let us look at the scriptures to confirm this fact:

> James 1 verse 13 *"Let no man say when he is tempted, I am tempted of God: for God cannot be tempted with evil, neither tempteth he any man: 14 But every man is tempted, when he is drawn away of his own lust, and enticed. 15 Then when lust hath conceived, it bringeth forth death. 16 Do not err, my beloved brethren. 17 Every GOOD AND PERFECT gift is from above, and cometh down from the Father of lights, with whom is no variableness, neither shadow of turning.* What more is there to say!

Point #2: God will not allow you to be tempted above which you are able.

Psalm 145:18, *The Lord is near to all who call upon Him, to all who call upon Him sincerely and in truth.*

Corinthians 10:13 *"There hath no temptation taken you but such as is common to man; but God is faithful who will not suffer you to be tempted above that you are able; but will with the temptation also make a way to escape, that you may be able to bear it.*

Romans 10:13, *For whosoever shall call upon the name of the Lord shall be saved"*

Point #3: God will always provide a way out of temptation.

Psalm 34:18 *The LORD is near to the broken-hearted; He saves the contrite in spirit. 19Many are the afflictions of the righteous, but the LORD delivers him from them all.*

Point #4: Your temptation is not unique, others have been where you are.

Keep this in mind, your temptation, test or trial is not unique, but common to man. What I mean by this is somebody else is, has, or will face the same challenge or challenges you're facing and all of them have been provided (by God), a way out. All who have trusted in Him and in His Word have found His escape route for them.

Jeremiah 17:7-8 *But blessed is the one who trust in the Lord, whose confidence is in him. They will be like a tree planted by the water that sends out its roots by the stream. It does not fear when heat comes; its leaves are always green. It has no worries in a year of drought and never fails to bear fruit".*

Isaiah 43:2 *When you pass through the waters, I will be with you; when you pass through the rivers, they will not sweep over you. When you walk through the fire, you will not be burned; the flames will not set you ablaze*

Chapter 5

————◦◉◦————

Persist to Resist

Jesus didn't resist temptation by ignoring the Tempter or the temptation. He opened up his mouth and spoke the written Word each time the devil approached him. We overcome the same way; by speaking God's word in faith.

Each time the devil tried to tempt Jesus, Jesus answered the temptation with the written Word of God. Jesus didn't keep silent, He didn't ignore the devil, He answered him with God's written Word. Some people, christian people, believe if you ignore the devil, he'll just go away. Let me ask you a question, if you ignore cancer, will it just go away? If you ignore heart disease, will it just go away? Well neither will the devil go away if you ignore him. If you ignore a cold, it can develop into the flu. And if you ignore the flu, it can develop into pneumonia and if you ignore pneumonia, it can kill you. No, you don't ignore the Tempter, Satan, or the temptation he tempts you with, you have to answer him with the written Word of God in the faith! God's Word doesn't say, "ignore the devil and he will flee from you, instead it says resist the devil and he will flee from you, James 4:7. I Peter 5:8,9 tells us how to resist him, it reads, "*Be sober, be vigilant, because your adversary the devil, as a roaring lion walketh about seeking whom he may devour 9 whom resist steadfast in the faith.* Ephesians 4:27 says, "*Neither give place to the devil.*

So, James 4:7 tells us to resist the devil (don't ignore him and don't entertain him). I Peter 5:8,9 further instructs us to be sober, be vigilant, and to resist steadfast (or by being strong) in the faith. Ephesians 4:27 instructs us to give no place to the devil (implying that he can only take what you give him by not resisting.

So the question now is: How do you go about resisting steadfast in the faith and giving no place to the devil? The answer is; by guarding the gates of your heart. What are the gates of your heart? The answer is; your eyes, your ears and your mouth.

Christians can avoid many temptations by guarding against what they see, what they hear and what they say. Your ears, your eyes and your mouth are gateways into your heart. In Proverbs 4:20-22, the writer addresses how we should guard our heart. It reads, "My son, attend to my words, incline your ear to my sayings, let them not depart out of your mouth, keep them in the midst of your heart, for they are life to all that find them and health to all their flesh. Psalm 119:105, tells us that God's word is a lamp unto our feet and a light unto our paths. Psalm 119:11 says, Your word have I hidden in my heart that I might not sin against you. The things you put before your eyes, allow into your ears and speaks from your mouth, will determine how successful you are at resisting the devil.

> Jesus said in Luke 6:47, 48, *As for everyone who comes to me and hears my words and puts them into practice, I will show you what they are like.They are like a man building a house, who dug down deep and laid the foundation on rock. When a flood came, the torrent struck that house but could not shake it, because it was well built.*

Before I move on, I want to give you a clearer picture of how to resist the devil. I Peter says we are to resist the devil steadfast in the faith, or by being strong in the faith. Well, Ephesians 6:10 tells us how; " Finally my brethren be strong in the Lord and in the power of his might. (Remember, Jesus is the Word made flesh). We can only be strong in the Lord; the Lord is Jesus Christ. Jesus is the Word). We might read it this way, Be strong in the Word. The only way to become strong in the Lord or in the Word, is to read, study, meditate on, confess, pray, and act upon the Word of God. *"Put on the whole armor of God, that you may be able to stand against the wiles (so that you can successfully resist all the devils methods. 12 For we wrestle not against flesh and blood, but against principalities, against powers, against the rulers of the darkness of this world, against spiritual wickedness in high places. 13 Wherefore take unto you the whole armor of God that you may be able to stand in the evil day (the day of temptation) and having done all to stand, 14 Stand therefore having your loins girt about with truth (buckle on the belt of Truth) having on the breastplate of righteousness 15 And your feet shod with the preparation of gospel of peace, (with the readiness to serve the Good News of peace as shoes for your feet. 16 And above all take the shield of faith where with you will be able to quench all the fiery darts of the wicked one (For with it you will be able to extinguish all the flaming darts of the evil one. 17 And take the helmet of salvation and the sword of the Spirit which is the Word of God. 18 Praying always with all prayer and supplications in the Spirit and watching thereunto with all perseverance and supplication for all the saints (give yourselves wholly to prayer and entreaty; pray on every occasion in the power of the Spirit and always on the alert to seize opportunities for doing so with unwearied persistence and entreaty on behalf of all the saints.*

This is the way to successfully resist the Devil. Later in the book, we will take a more in depth look at the "Whole Armor of God"

It is an absolute fact that the born again believer can live a sin-free life. This does not mean he is never confronted by sin, sin will always confront him, but, now that he is In Christ, sin no longer has power over him. Living a sin-free life doesn't mean a believer won't ever slip and sin. It means that if he slips into it, he doesn't have to stay there; he doesn't have to camp out in sin. It means that we are no longer sin's slaves. Here is how this whole thing works: I John chapter 1 beginning at verse 8, *"If we say that we have no sin, we deceive ourselves and there is no truth in us. 9 But if we confess our sins (to God), He is faithful and just to forgive us our* sins, and to cleanse us from all unrighteousness. Now take a look at I John 2:1,2, "My little children, these things I write unto you, that ye sin not. And if any man sin, we have an advocate with the Father, Jesus Christ the righteous: 2 And he is the propitiation (restorer of fellowship or favor with God) for our sins: and not for ours only, but also for the sins of the whole world.

Because we are no longer slaves to sin, Sin is not our master! A slave is always conscious of his master. The slave's consciousness of his master compels him to please his master continually whether he desires to or not. A slave does what he is told without the consideration of options, for he has none! Sin is unrighteousness. Well, Jesus has made us free from sins lordship over us. We are no longer slaves to sin, we are the righteousness of God in Christ Jesus. Jesus Christ himself has been made our Righteousness. Righteousness has now become our master. When we were sinners, Sin was our master and we were conscious of it. Now Christ is our Righteousness and He is our master. We must become conscious of Him and his Righteousness which He has imputed (attributed or ascribed) to us.

Becoming Righteousness conscious is something we have to do on purpose. Because of Adam's sin against God, we were all born into sin and sin's nature. When we receive salvation by receiving Jesus into our hearts; when we are born again, we are born unto God and we take on His nature. When we took upon us His nature, our spirits were recreated; made brand new, regenerated. We become brand new creations! The moment we believed in Jesus Christ and asked Him to come into our hearts by faith, we received Him as our personal Lord and Savior and at that very moment he inhabited our hearts. At that very moment, we received His life, His nature and His ability. II Corinthians 5:17, *Therefore if any man be in Christ, he is a new creation, old things are passed away, behold all things are made new.*

Galatians 2:20 *I have been crucified with Christ; it is no longer I who live, but Christ who lives in me and the life that I now live in the flesh, I live by the faith of the Son of God who loved me and gave himself for me.*

Why Do I Struggle?

So, if I have become a new creation, why do I still struggle with sin? This is a question many Christians ask. Because of a lack of understanding many are led to believe they still possess their old nature; that the old nature and new nature are to co-exist and that the battle between the two is just a fact of the life of the Christian. The danger of this misconception is a lifetime deprivation of victorious living. Remember II Cor 5:17, *Therefore if any man be in Christ, he is a new creation, old things are passed away, behold all things are made new.*

Ephesians 4:22 instructs us to put off our former way of life, the old self, which is being corrupted by its deceitful desires; 23 be renewed in the spirit of our minds; 24 and to put on the new self, created to be like God in true righteousness and holiness.

If one believes he has no power over sin; or that he is forever a sinner, he will never rise to a place of spiritual maturity and go on to do the works of Jesus. Jesus said,

"He that believeth in me, the works that I do he will do and greater works he will do also, for I go to my Father".

If we believe we can never overcome sin, then as far as we're concerned, all that Jesus did on the cross was in vain. If we do not believe we are masters over sin, we will forever live with a sin consciousness that will hinder us from assuming our roles as sons of God!

Chapter 6

Understanding the Nature of Man;
The Process of Change;
The New Life in Christ.

We learn from I Thessalonians 5:23 that man is a three-fold being; spirit, soul and body. Man is a spirit, he possesses a soul and he lives in a body. Man's spirit is the real or true man. When man is born again, it is his spirit that is recreated and made brand new. His spirit has taken on the nature and likeness of God. In fact God Himself has come to make His home in us. Man's body is the house that the true man, the spirit of man, lives in. The body or flesh is not born again, it remains the same. It desires to do all the things it did before the spirit was reborn. It still has all the desires, habits, etc. it had before. The soul of man on the other hand, is made up of man's mind, will and emotions. The mind acts as an umpire. It determines the outcome of the actions and behavior of man when confronted with sin.

When man is born again, his spirit is made brand new instantly, however there is a transformation that has to take place in order for the total man, spirit soul and body to line up with the new creation. This transformation can only take place by the renewing of the mind with the Word of God, otherwise the body's determination to continue its habit of satisfying itself will overcome the total man's desire to live for God. Romans 12:2 *And be ye not conformed to this world: but be ye transformed by the renewing of your mind, that ye may prove what is that good, and acceptable and perfect will of God*

This is how we overcome sin: Put off the old, put on the new:

Ephesians 4:22-24 *That you put off, concerning your former conduct, the old man which grows corrupt according to the deceitful lust, 23 and be renewed in the spirit of your mind, 24 and that you put on the new man which was created according to God, in true righteousness and holiness.*

In everything pertaining to the kingdom of God, there is always a God-side and a Man-side. God has a part to play and man has a part to play. God has already done his part as He has provided for a life of victory for mankind. He sent his Son Jesus Christ to die on the cross for our sins so that we might be made right with him; so that we might once again fellowship with him. Because of what Jesus has done on our behalf we can come boldly into the Father's presence without the feeling of guilt or inferiority. We can live overcoming lives! He has taken away sins power or lordship over us. He won the victory over the evil one, stripped him of his authority, led captivity captive and gave us gifts that would help us to overcome every effort of Satan to rule over us. We were Satans slaves; held hopelessly in bondage to sin, but not anymore, for whom the Son sets free is free indeed!! We are free!

This freedom is not the freedom to just exist, but the freedom to rule and reign over the evil forces that once held us bound. Jesus said in Luke 10:19, *Behold I give you authority to tread upon serpents and scorpions and over all the power of the enemy and nothing by any means harm you*". He also said in Mark's gospel chapter 16:15-18, "*Go into all the world and preach the gospel to every creature. 16 He who believes and is baptized shall be saved; but he who does not believe will be condemned. 17 "And these signs shall follow those who believe: In my name they will cast out demons; they will speak with new tongues; 18"They will take up serpents; and if they drink anything deadly, it will by no means hurt them; they will lay hands on the sick and they will recover"*. THIS is the freedom that our Father God wants us to live in. One cannot live in freedom and in bondage at the same time. Either he is free or he is not. Whom the Son has made free is free indeed!

Many Christians interpret the passage of scripture in Romans chapter 7 in a way they believe supports the fact that the struggle with sin is hopeless. Let's take a look at it now.

Romans 7:15-25 GOD'S WORD Translation (GW)

> *15 I don't realize what I'm doing. I don't do what I want to do. Instead, I do what I hate. 16 I don't do what I want to do, but I agree that God's standards are good. 17 So I am no longer the one who is doing the things I hate, but sin that lives in me is doing them.*
>
> *18 I know that nothing good lives in me; that is, nothing good lives in my corrupt nature. Although I have the desire to do what is right, I don't do it. 19 I don't do the good I want to do. Instead, I do the evil that I don't want to do. 20 Now, when I do what I don't want to do, I am no longer the one who is doing it. Sin that lives in me is doing it.*

21 So I've discovered this truth: Evil is present with me even when I want to do what God's standards say is good. 22 I take pleasure in God's standards in my inner being. 23 However, I see a different standard at work throughout my body. It is at war with the standards my mind sets and tries to take me captive to sin's standards which still exist throughout my body. 24 What a miserable person I am! Who will rescue me from my dying body? 25 I thank God that our Lord Jesus Christ rescues me! So I am obedient to God's standards with my mind, but I am obedient to sin's standards with my corrupt nature.

So many times I have heard teachings that use these passages to support the christians hopeless efforts to overcome sin; oftentimes leaving hearers with a sense of defeat and reinforcing or even elevating their consciousness of sin and its mastery over their lives. When the Apostle Paul wrote this letter, he did not write it as a stand alone scripture. In fact, none of the original texts of scriptures were written in chapter and verse. This portion of the Apostle Paul's letter is a part of a complete letter that can only be fully understood by reading the entire book of Romans and especially chapters 6 and 8. So that we can forever put to rest any speculation that the Christian's battle with sin is a hopeless one, I am adding these chapters for inspection so that you can see for yourself what the Holy Spirit was saying to us through the inspired scriptures penned by Paul the Apostle.

> Romans 6:1 " *What shall we say then? Shall we continue to live in sin so that God's grace will increase? 2 Certainly not! We have died to sin. How then can we go on living in it? 3 For surely you know that when we were baptized into union with Christ Jesus, we were baptized into union with his death. 4 By our baptism, then, we were buried with him and shared his death, in order that, just as Christ was raised from death by the glorious power of the Father, so also we might live a new life. 5 For since we have become one with him in dying as he did, in the same way we shall be one with him by being raised to life as he was. 6 And we know that our being has been put to death with Christ on his cross, in order that the power of the sinful self might be destroyed, so that we should no longer be the slaves of sin. 7 For when we die, we are set free from the power of sin. 8 Since we have died with Christ, we believe that we will also live with him. 9 For we know that Christ has been raised from death and will never die again - death will no longer rule over him. 10 And so, because he died, sin has no power over him; and now he lives his life in fellowship with*

God. In the same way you are to think of your-selves as dead, so far as sin is concerned, but living in fellowship with God through Christ Jesus. 12 Sin must no longer rule in your mortal bodies, so that you obey the desires of your nat-ural self. 13 Nor must you surrender any part of yourselves to sin to be used for wicked pur-poses. Instead, give yourselves to God, as those who have been brought from death to life, and surrender your whole being to him to be used for righteous purposes. 14 Sin must not be your master; for you do not live under law but under God's grace.

15 What, then? Shall we sin, because we are not under law but under God's grace? By no means! 16 Surely you know that when you surrender yourselves as slaves to obey someone you are in fact the slaves of the master you obey — of sin, which results in death, or of obedience, which results in being put right with God. 17 But thanks be to God! For though at one time you were slaves to sin, you have obeyed with all your heart the truth found in the teaching you received. 18 You were set free from sin and became slaves of righteousness. 19 (I use everyday language because of the weakness of your natural selves.) At one time you surren-dered yourselves entirely as slaves to impurity and wickedness for wicked purposes. In the same way you must now surrender yourselves entirely as slaves of righteousness of holy purposes. 20 When you were the slaves of sin, you were free from righteousness. 21 What did you gain from doing the things that you are now ashamed of? The result of those things is death! 22 But now you have been set free from sin and are the slaves of God. Your gain is a life fully dedicated to him, and the result is eternal life. 23 For sin pays its wage—death; but God's free gift is eternal life in union with Christ Jesus our Lord.

I realized we covered the entire 6th chapter of Romans, but I make no apologies because the scriptures do a much better job than we do in communicating God Word!

Chapter 6 of Romans precedes chapter 7, and so sets the stage for the thought the Apostle Paul is communicating in chapter 7 which seems to be a hopeless cry from a man who is trapped in his sinful condition, when it is not read in context.

Chapter 7

———◦◉◦———

The Rest Of The Story

N ow I want us to take a look at the entire chapter of Romans chapter 8. I would like to note the caption in my Thompson Chain Reference Study Bible at the beginning of the chapter: "Free From Indwelling Sin". It also notes the five major emphasis of this chapter:

1. There is no condemnation to those in Christ Jesus (v1)

2. The Spirit delivers from the power of the flesh (v2) 3. The Spirit authenticates sonship (v12)

4. The Spirit assures future glory (v18)

5. The Spirit assures final victory (v31)

Romans 8:1 *There is therefore now no condemnation to those who are in Christ Jesus, who do not walk according to the flesh, but according to the Spirit. 2 For the law of the Spirit of life in Christ Jesus has made us free from the law of sin and death. 3 For what the law could not do in that it was weak through the flesh God did by sending His own Son In the likeness of sinful flesh, on the account of sin: He condemned sin in the flesh, 4 that the righteous requirement of the law might be fulfilled in us who do not walk according to the flesh, but according to the Spirit. 5 For those who live according to the flesh set their minds on the things of the flesh, but those who live according to the Spirit, the things of the Spirit. 6 For to be carnally minded is death, but to be spiritually minded is life and peace. 7Because the carnal mind is enmity (hostile) against God, for it is not subject to the law of God nor indeed can be. 8 So then, those who are in the flesh cannot please God. 9But you are not in the flesh but in the Spirit if indeed the Spirit of God dwells in you. Now if anyone does not have the Spirit of Christ, he is not His. 10 And if Christ is in you, the body is dead because of sin, but the Spirit is life because of righteousness 11 But if the Spirit of Him who raised Jesus from the dead dwells in you, He who raised Christ from the dead will also give life to your mortal bodies through His Spirit who dwells in you.*

12 Therefore brethren, we are debtors—not of the flesh, to live according to the flesh. 13 For if you live according to the flesh you will die; but if through the Spirit, you put to death the deeds of the body, you will live. 14 For as many as are led by the Spirit of God, these are sons of God. 15 For you did not receive the spirit of bondage again to fear, but you received the Spirit of adoption by who we cry out "Abba Father." 16 The Spirit Himself bears witness with our spirit that we are children of God, 17 and if children, then heirs—heirs of God and joint heirs with Christ, if indeed we suffer with Him, that we may also be glorified together.

Contrary to the seemingly hopeless struggle with sin as expressed in Romans chapter 7 when isolated from the rest of his letter, Paul tells us in Chapter 8 that we are very much empowered to win over sin and he tells us how to win every time. He says that for those who are in Christ Jesus, who walk after the spirit and who mind the things of the Spirit, we will live a life free of sin and of sin's condemnation. But those who walk after the flesh, and do mind the things of the flesh will not enjoy life or peace. In fact he says to be carnally minded is death (separation from God), and the carnal mind is incapable of pleasing God.

Faith pleases God!

Life and peace come from fellowship and sweet communion with the Father. Carnality interrupts that fellowship robbing one of God's supply of joy and peace. It compromises the confidence of one's standing with the Father who invites us to approach his throne boldly. It robs one of his consciousness of sonship and the hope or the confident expectation necessary to receive from God when we pray. The Bible tells us that the just (those who have been justified or made right with God by the blood of Jesus) shall live by faith. While Faith is the substance of things hoped for and the evidence of things not seen as noted in Heb. 11:1 ; Hope is the confident expectation that first of all; God hears your prayers and secondly, that he will answer them. This is the confidence we have in Him, that when we pray He hears us, and because we know He hears us, we know we have the petitions we desire of Him. (I John 5:14). If we live a life of carnality, we lose the sense of confidence. We become timid in our approach to God, uncertain of His attention to our prayers and unsure if He will answer even if He hears us. Thus, the struggle to find confidence, peace, or joy by the one who lives according to the flesh will be fruitless until or unless he yields himself to his recreated spirit which of God has been created unto righteousness.

The Apostle John expresses the Father's will regarding sin in I John 2:1. *He writes, "My little children these things write I unto you that ye sin not...*

The Apostle Paul says it this way in Romans 12:1, *"I beseech ye brethren by the mercies of God that ye present your bodies a living sacrifice, holy and acceptable to God which is your reasonable (spiritual) service. 2 And be not conformed to this world, but be ye transformed by the renewing of your mind that you may prove what is that good and acceptable and perfect will of God."*

> Here's how sin attempts to rob you of God's best for your life; In order to prove what is that good and acceptable and perfect will of God for your life you must know what His will is. And in order for you to know what his will is, you must fellowship with Him. In order to fellowship with Him, you must approach Him. In order to approach Him, you must have confidence in the fact that when you call on Him, He will hear you and answer you and give you the things you desire of Him.

Sin consciousness takes away the confidence we need to approach God as a son. It causes men to shy away from God even though He invites us to come boldly before His throne so that we might obtain mercy and find grace to help in the time of need.

Sin consciousness causes men to draw back from God. It is this drawing back from God that displeases Him. Hebrews 10:38 - *Now the just shall live by faith, but if any man draws back, my soul hath no pleasure in him.* Heb 11:6 says, "*But without faith it is impossible to please Him (God) for he that cometh to God must believe that he is and that he is a rewarder of them that diligently seeks Him.*

We all agree that everything we need in life comes from God. We also agree that in order to receive from God we must go to him and ask him for whatever we need. God's word tells us that when we go to Him, we must go believing two (2) things: 1. That HE IS. 2. That He is a rewarder of them that diligently seek him. I John 5:14 says, " And this is the confidence that we have in him, that if we ask anything according to His will, he hears us: 15 And if we know that he hears us, whatsoever we ask, we know that we have the petitions that we desire of him"

The Apostle John says our confidence is in the fact that we know when we ask anything according to His will

He hears us, and if we know He hears us we know we have whatever we desire of Him.

This confidence or faith we must have in order to receive from God can only come as a result of knowing, or being confident that we are in right standing with the Father; that we are righteous. Being conscious of your righteousness or right standing with God will give you the boldness you need to, first of all, approach the throne of God and secondly to leave the throne room knowing that you have what you've asked of Him.

> Mark 11:22, *"Have faith in God 23 For verily I say unto you that whosoever shall say unto this mountain be removed and be cast into the sea and shall not doubt in his heart but shall believe that whatsoever he saith shall come to pass, he shall have whatsoever he saith. 24 Therefore whatsoever things you desire when you pray, believe you receive them and you shall have them.*

Now let's read Mark 11:22 in light of Hebrews 11:6.. Have faith in God by coming to Him believing that He is and that He is a rewarder of those that diligently seek Him...

Let's read it in light of I John 5:14. Have faith in God by having this confidence in Him that if we ask anything according to his will he hears us: and since we know he hears us, we know we have the petitions we desire of him.

Sin consciousness will rob you of your confidence, thus robbing you of the blessings of God. Your understanding of righteousness will give you the confidence you need in order to approach God and to take hold of the promises He has provided for us in His redemption of man through the blood of Jesus.

Do you remember how Adam and Eve, after they had sinned, hid from God when they heard his voice as he came walking through the garden in the cool of the day? Let's take a look at it in Gen. 3:8 *"And they heard the voice of the Lord walking in the garden in the cool of the day and Adam and his wife hid themselves from the presence of the Lord amongst the trees of the garden. 9 And God called unto Adam and said unit him, where art thou? 10 And he said I heard thy voice in the garden and I was afraid because I was naked: and I hid myself. 11 And he (God) said who told thee that thou was naked? Hast thou eaten of the tree whereof I commanded thee the thou shouldest not eat?*

God had given Adam a commandment. Gen 2:15 *And the Lord commanded them saying, Of the tree of the knowledge of good Good and Evil thou shall not eat of it for in the day thou latest thereof thou shalt surely die."*

In verse 17 when God told Adam he would surely die on the day he ate of the tree of the knowledge of good and evil, that is exactly what happened! Adam immediately died a spiritual death, and eventually died a physical death. Adam lived to be nine hundred and thirty years old, but he died. That was not God's plan for him. God created man to live forever and never die.

Death was introduced into the world when Adam sinned by disobeying God's commandment. John 5:12, *"Wherefore as by one man (Adam) sin entered into the world and death by sin; and so death passed upon all men, for that all have sinned.*

Spiritual death is separation from God. The moment Adam and Eve ate of the fruit of the tree of the knowledge of good and evil in the garden; they, because of their disobedience, were immediately separated from the sweet fellowship they once enjoyed with God their Father. Before Adam and Eve disobeyed God, they were clothed with the Righteousness of God. God had created them in His righteous image so there was nothing that stood between them, there was nothing to prevent Adam's sweet fellowship with His Father. Adam enjoyed a sweet uninterrupted union with God. By disobeying God's commandment, Adam and Eve sinned and the righteousness with which they were clothed was removed; Before they sinned they were clothed with God's righteousness, After they sinned they became unclothed or unrighteous. Adams' decision to disobey God resulted in sin's entrance into the world and death accompanied it.

Adam and Eve were naked because their sin robbed them of their righteousness or their right standing with God. They were no longer like God so when they heard Him walking in the garden, they hid from Him. Sin had brought darkness into their lives, and darkness reigned until the law came which helped man to see their sins but could never take them away. From the time Adam and Eve sinned, the sacrifice of innocent animals had to be made in order to cover man's sins. This was a type and shadow of the ultimate sacrifice that would have to be made by God's own Son as He would later shed His own blood to take away the sins of man cleansing him from unrighteousness and restoring his righteousness or right standing with the Father.

Romans 5:12-21 explains the restoration of man's righteousness. It reads:

> **12** *Therefore, just as sin entered the world through one man, and death through sin,and in this way death came to all people, because all sinned—*

> **13** *To be sure, sin was in the world before the law was given, but sin is not charged against*

*anyone's account where there is no law. **14** Nevertheless, death reigned from the time of Adam to the time of Moses, even over those who did not sin by breaking a command, as did Adam, who is a pattern of the one to come.*

***15** But the gift is not like the trespass. For if the many died by the trespass of the one man, how much more did God's grace and the gift that came by the grace of the one man, Jesus Christ, overflow to the many! **16** Nor can the gift of God be compared with the result of one man's sin: The judgment followed one sin and brought condemnation, but the gift followed many trespasses and brought justification. **17** For if, by the trespass of the one man, death reigned through that one man, how much more will those who receive God's abundant provision of grace and of the gift of righteousness reign in life through the one man, Jesus Christ!*

***18** Consequently, just as one trespass resulted in condemnation for all people, so also one righteous act resulted in justification and life for all people. **19** For just as through the disobedience of the one man the many were made sinners, so also through the obedience of the one man the many will be made righteous.*

20 *The law was brought in so that the trespass might increase. But where sin increased, grace increased all the more,* **21** *so that, just as sin reigned in death, so also grace might reign through righteousness to bring eternal life through Jesus Christ our Lord.*

In other words, ADAM MESSED IT UP; THE LAW PATCHED IT UP; BUT JESUS FIXED IT UP! Glory be to God!

Chapter 8

God Is Not Mad At You

When I was a child I saw a painting that etched an image of God in my mind that had me very confused about what our relationship with Him should look like. In the painting, the artist portrayed God as a white-haired, long bearded man. He was positioned in the top left hand corner of the painting, in the sky or the heavens. In his hand, he held a lightning bolt. In the bottom right hand corner of the painting was a man. God was pointing the lightning bolt at the man as though he was just waiting on the man to make the wrong move so that he could hurl it at him. I don't know about others who saw the painting, but I had a hard time seeing the loving, fatherly, patient, kind, temperate, forgiving nature of God in that picture. In fact when I thought about God in light of that picture, it frightened me and certainly discouraged me from the very idea of approaching Him. Even the thought of serving Him was one that would be motivated by fear. It was easy to imagine when people would say, "God is going to punish you, and I heard that a lot, that He was going to do just that! So for me God was a punishing God, an angry God, a scary God! He wasn't someone I wanted to draw near to but rather someone I wanted to steer clear of!

And to be honest with you, I really felt a bit hopeless. Think about it, according to most of the people I was surrounded by, and I mean good church-going folks, either the devil was going to get me; or God was going to punish me! I just couldn't win! I'm telling you I would try my best not to do anything wrong because I didn't want the devil to get me or God to punish me. But, it seemed the harder I tried to do the right, the more wrong I did. I'd do one right thing and then two wrong things. I had been taught that it's only when you do everything right, that you get to go to heaven, but when you did anything wrong you were going to hell. So of course I tried to do everything right. I'd be heading for heaven one weak and to hell the next. I wanted to do right all the time but I just couldn't, so finally I'd just give up. Then later on sometimes a week or so, sometimes a month, sometimes six months, and sometimes I would go for a year before even attempting to get back on track.

When I became a teenager I read about David in the Bible. David seemed to have found favor in the sight of

God. He seemed to have known the tender side of God. God called David a man after His own heart. This is what I wanted. I desired to be like David, a man after God's own heart. However, I was a little confused about how David could be a man after God's own heart, or be favored by God when he was obviously not a perfect man. David was the king of Israel, God's chosen people. King David, slept with another man's wife. When she told David she was pregnant with his child, he tried to cover it up by first attempting to manipulate the woman's husband to sleep with her so that the husband would think he had fathered the child. After his plan failed, he had the man, a loyal servant in King David's army, murdered and made it look like just another casualty of war.

Come on! How in the world could God approve of this man David? But He did! And so I thought to myself, if God could forgive David, He could forgive me. If God could love David, He could certainly love me. If David could become a man after God's own heart, so could I!

In looking at David's life, I see three things in particular that I believe made David a man after God's Heart:

1. God chose him

2. David had a repentant heart and repented of his sin

3. David lived a lifestyle of Praise and Worship

Here's the parallel:

1. God chose us

2. God forgives us when we repent

3. God inhabits our praise when we praise and worship him.

As I began to read the Bible more I found out that David and I had a lot in common. Let me show you what I mean:

1. God chose David.

2. You can read the story of how Saul was rejected by God because of his disobedience and how God chose David to become king of Israel in II Samuel the fifteenth and sixteenth chapters. Well the Bible says in Ephesians 1:4 that God has chosen us also! Eph 1:3, 4 says, *"Blessed be the God and Gather of our Lord Jesus Christ who has blessed us with all spiritual blessings in heavenly places in Christ 4 according as he has chosen us IN HIM from the foundation of the world, that we should be holy and without blame before him in love 5 Having predestined us unto the adoption of children by Jesus Christ unto himself according to the good pleasure*

of his will. To the praise of the glory of his grace wherein he has made us accepted in the Beloved (Christ Jesus).

You might say, "But God chose David to be a king." *That's true, and he has also chosen us to be kings and priests. Revelation 1:4, "unto Him that loved us and washed us from our sins in His own blood 6 And has made us kings and priests unto God and His Father; to him be glory and dominion forever and ever, amen.*

I Peter 2:9, *"But you are a chosen generation, a royal priesthood, a holy nation that you should show forth the praises of him that called you out of darkness into his marvelous light.*

So God chose David, but He has also chosen me and He's chosen you!

3.   David repented of his sins and God forgave him.

When we repent of our sins, God forgives us too! I John 1:9, *"If we confess our sins he (God) is faithful and just to forgive our sins and to cleanse us of all unrighteousness. Ephesians 1:7, "In whom (Jesus) we have redemption through his blood, the forgiveness of sins according to the riches of his grace. II Corinthians 5:21, For He (God the Father) hath made him (Christ Jesus) to*

69

be sin for us who knew no sin that we might be made
the righteousness of God in Him".

4.   David lived a life of praise and worship.

David was a man after God's own heart! David was a
man who was in pursuit of God's heart. He pursued
God on purpose. He sought the heart of God. David
fellowshipped with God out of desire, not out of duty.

In Psalm 42:1 we get a glimpse of this: *"As the
hart (deer) panteth after the water brooks, so
panteth my soul after thee of God 2 My soul
thirst for God, for the living God: when shall I
come and appear before God.*

Psalm 18:1, *"I will love thee, O Lord, my strength.
2 The Lord is my rock and my fortress and my
deliverer, my God, my strength, in him I will
trust, my buckler and the horn of my salvation
and my high tower.*

Ps 28:1, *" Unto thee will I cry O Lord my rock:
be not silent to me lest if thou be silent to me,
I become like them that go down into the pit.*

David's sensitivity to God gave him the ability to rule
God's people according to God's desire. He sought God
for the direction, wisdom, protection and strength

he needed to effectively lead the nation of Israel, God's chosen people. So David lived a life that was pleasing to God!

Like David I can make my life one of praise and thanksgiving on purpose. The Bible tells us in I Peter 2:5 that we are built up as living stones, we are built up as a spiritual house, a holy priesthood to offer up spiritual sacrifices acceptable to God by Jesus Christ. In the same chapter of I Peter in verse 9, the scriptures tell us that we are a chosen generation, a royal priesthood, a holy nation, a peculiar people that we should show forth the praises of him who has called us out of darkness into his marvelous light:

So God tells us in His word that not only should we voice our praise of God, but that we should also show forth the praises of Him. This word "praises" in this verse is actually translated virtues. It is also translated, "excellence". So he says we should show forth the excellence of him who hath called us out of darkness into his marvelous light.

> Psalm 8:1 *David says, "O Lord, our Lord how excellent is thy name in all the earth; who has set thy glory above the heavens."*

Psalm 148:13 *Let them praise the name of the Lord for his name alone is excellent: his glory is above heaven and earth.*

Psalm 150:2 *Praise him for His mighty acts, praise him according to his excellent greatness.* In Psalm 22:3 David says, "*But thou art holy, O thou that inhabits the praises of Israel*

The last four chapters in the Book of Psalms, chapters, 145, 146, 147, 148, 149 and 150, are all about Praising God. It would do us good to spend some time reading these chapters.

How does one live a lifestyle of praise? Deuteronomy 10:12 says,"

1. Fear (revere) the Lord thy God

2. Walk in all His ways

3. Love Him

4. Serve Him with all your heart and all your soul

5. Keep His commandments and statues.

I know that it seems like a lot to do; keeping all his commandments; and it is, or was! So Jesus made it simpler for us under the new Covenant or New Law to walk in obedience to all God's commandments. Galatians 5:6 reads, *"For all the law is fulfilled in one word, even in this, 'Thou shalt love thy neighbor as thyself.'"*

Romans 13:8 *Owe no man anything but to love one another for he that loveth another hath fulfilled the law. 9 For this thou shalt not commit adultery, thou shalt not kill, thou shall not steal, thou shalt not bear false witness, and if there be any commandment it is briefly comprehended in this saying, namely, thou shalt love thy neighbor as thyself. 10 Love worketh no ill to his neighbor therefore love is the fulfilling of the Law.*

Chapter 9

———◆———

God's Gift That Keeps On Giving

Righteousness is the ability to stand in the presence of God without the feeling of guilt or inferiority; without the feeling of unworthiness. It is the ability to stand in the presence of God as though you never sinned. The righteousness of God is His gift to us. It is the righteousness OF GOD, or God's own righteousness. Not man's righteousness, God's righteousness! It is a gift that cannot be obtained by good works on man's part. Jesus, God's Son, became sin for us that we might be MADE the righteousness of God in Him. The moment we accept Jesus Christ as our personal Lord and Savior, we are made righteous. This is an unlimited righteousness. Righteousness cannot be measured in degrees. You don't become more righteous or less righteous. Righteousness does not increase or decrease. Your righteousness does not grow. When Jesus made man became as righteous as he will ever be..

Righteousness does not grow, Righteousness has fruit and the fruit of righteousness does grow. Isaiah 32:17 refers to the fruit of righteousness as the work of Righteousness and the effect of righteousness. Is 32:17. *And the work of righteousness shall be peace and the effectiveness of righteousness, quietness and assurance forever.*

The Apostle Paul writes in his letter to the church of believers at Philippi in Phillipians 1:9-11,

And it is my prayer that your love may abound more and more in knowledge and discernment so that you may approve, what is excellent and be pure and blameless for the day of Christ, filled with the fruit of righteousness that comes through Jesus Christ, to the glory and praise of God.

Righteousness doesn't grow, but the fruits of righteousness does. A better way to say this is: The state of righteousness can't grow, but the fruit of righteousness can and should; God expects for it to.

The fruit of Righteousness will not grow automatically. It has to be cultivated, maintained, nurtured and guarded. The way to do this is found in the scriptures in I Peter 2:1, "*Wherefore laying aside all malice, and all evil, no more lying, or hypocrisy or jealousy or insulting language., 2 Be like newborn babies, always thirsty for the spiritual milk, so that by drinking it you may grow up.*

Jesus's provision for the growth and development of the fruit of righteousness can be found in Ephesians 4 verses 11-16 "*And he gave some apostles, some prophets, some evangelists, some pastors and some teachers. He did this to prepare all God's people for the work of Christian service in order to build up the body of Christ. 3 And so we shall all come together to that oneness in our faith and in our knowledge of the Son of God; we shall become mature people reaching to the very height of Christ's full stature.*

Then we shall no longer be children carried by waves and blown about by every shifting wind of teaching of deceitful people who lead others into error but the tricks they invent. Instead speaking the truth in a spirit of love, we must grow up in every way to Christ who is the Head. Under His control all the different parts of the body fit together and the whole body is held together by every joint with which it is provided. So when each separate part works as it should, the whole body grows and builds itself up through love.

So in and through these scriptures we can see clearly God's plan for us regarding the expansion of His kingdom throughout the earth. The Apostle Paul was called by God, and from God received the revelation of Righteousness so that he might share this revelation with the Body of Christ both in his day and through his epistles or letters to the churches, throughout the entire church age.

> Paul writes in Ephesians 3:8-12, *"Unto me who am less than the least of all the saints is this grace given that I should preach among the Gentiles the unsearchable riches of Christ. 9 And to make all men see what is the fellowship of the mystery which from the beginning of the world had been hid in God who created all things by Jesus Christ. 10 To the intent that now unto principalities and powers in heavenly places might be known by the church the manifold wisdom of God. 11 According to the eternal purpose which he proposed in Christ Jesus our Lord. 12 In whom we have boldness and access with confidence by the faith of Him.*

In his letter to the believers at the church in Colossae, Paul writes of the mandate given to him by God to share this revelation of Righteousness with the Church: Colossians 1:25-28. *"Wherefore I am made a minister according to the dispensation of God which is given to me for you to fulfill the Word of God:*

26 Even the mystery which had been hidden from the ages and from generations but now is made manifest to his saints 27 To whom God would make known the glory of this mystery among the Gentiles: which is Christ in you the hope of glory. 28 Whom we preach, warning every man and teaching every man in all wisdom; that we may present every man perfect (mature) in Christ Jesus.

The Good News Translation of verse 28 reads, *"So we preach Christ to everyone. With all possible wisdom we warn and teach them in order to bring each one into God's presence, a mature individual in union with Christ."*

In essence God's plan for Paul's life and ministry was to help each Christian believer to grow up spiritually.

Remember Jesus's prayer as recorded in John 17:20-23,

"Neither pray I for these alone, but for them also which shall believe on me through their word; 21 That they all may be one as thou, Father, art in me, and I in thee, that they also may be one in us: that the world may believe that thou hast sent me. 22 And the glory which thou gavest me I have given them; that they may be one, even as we are one: 23 I in them, and thou in me,

*that they may be made perfect in one and that
the world may know that thou hast sent me,
and hast loved them, as thou hast loved me."*

Jesus' prayer to the Father was that we would come
into perfect union with Him even as He is in perfect
union with the Father. Our union with Him, unites us
with the Father. Our union with Him serves as a tes-
timony to the world that God the Father sent Christ
Jesus into the world.

Now pay close attention to verse 22 of John 17, "*And
the glory which thou gavest me I have given them;
that they may be one, even as we are one: 23, "I in
them, and thou in me, that they may be made perfect (complete) in one and that the world may know
(through their union with me, by the glory I have given
them, which is the same glory you have given me), that
thou hast sent me, and has loved them, as thou hast
loved me."*

I want us to take a look at what Jesus is saying here in
light of Ephesians chapter two beginning at the first
verse: NIV Translation

*1 And you He made alive, who were dead in
trespasses and sins 2 in which you once walked
according to the course of this world, according
to the prince of the power of the air, the spirit*

who now works in the sons of disobedience, 3 among whom also we all once conducted ourselves in the lust of our flesh, fulfilling the desires of the flesh and of the mind, and were by nature children of wrath, just as the others. 4 But God, who is rich in mercy, because of His great love with which He loved us, 5 even when we were dead in trespasses, made us alive together with Christ (by grace you have been saved), 6 and raised us up together, and made us sit together in the heavenly places in Christ Jesus. 7 that in ages to come He might show the exceeding riches of His grace in His kindness towards us in Christ Jesus. 8 For by grace have you been saved through faith, and that not of yourselves; it is the gift of God, 9 not of works, lest anyone should boast. 10. For we are His workmanship, created in Christ Jesus for good works, which God prepared beforehand that we should walk in them."

How do I help people to become mature Christians?

As co-laborers with Jesus Christ, we can help people to grow spiritually by helping them to see, through scriptures like Ephesians 3:12. that in Christ they can all have boldness and access with confidence by the faith of Him (God). In other words, every born again believer may boldly and confidently approach God in prayer and fellowship. To approach God boldly does not mean to approach Him arrogantly or irreverently. Instead, it means to approach Him with the confidence that you are in His presence at His invitation which is always open to you because you are His child. Our approach should always be with reverence, thanksgiving and praise because He is God, and He is our Father.

This confidence I speak of is not confidence in ourselves, but rather faith in what Jesus did on our behalf on Calvary's cross, in that He removed forever that veil that once separated us from our Father God. Because Christ now lives in us, when we approach the throne of God, we do not approach it alone, Christ is in us and God sees us in the face of Jesus.

> Remember we read in Galatians 2:20 KJV "*I am crucified with Christ, nevertheless I live yet not I, but Christ lives in me, and the life that I now live in the flesh, I live by the faith of the Son of God who loved me and gave himself for me*"

The Apostle Paul said that the riches of the glory of God's mystery which was hidden in the past but has since been revealed is this; Christ is in us and this is our hope (or confident expectation) of glory. Christ, who has been made unto us righteousness, lives in us. He is our Righteousness and God has made us (through Jesus' work at calvary, the Righteousness of God in Him; we've been MADE righteous through His blood.

Chapter 10

Fruit Bearers

God wants us to grow up and to become mature Christians. He needs us to grow up and to become mature Christians. Why? Because of what Jesus said in the Gospels of John 15:16, *"Ye have not chosen me, but I have chosen you and ordained you, that ye should go and bring forth fruit and that your fruit should remain.*

Jesus wants us to be fruit bearers. Baby Christians don't bear much fruit. Bearing fruit glorifies God our Father. In John 15:8, *Jesus said, "Herein is my Father glorified, that you bear much fruit, so shall you be my disciples. Fruit bearing is proof of being disciples of Christ.*

A Disciple is a follower of Christ. How do we follow Him? In John 14:12, *Jesus said, "Verily, Verily I say unto you, he that believeth on me, the works I do, he shall do also and greater works than these shall he do because I go unto my father.*

Mature Christians do the works that Jesus did. Jesus' works were not his own works, but the works or the will of the Father. John 6:38, *"For I have come down, from heaven, not to do mine own will, but the will of Him who sent me"*

The "Works" as it relates to righteousness is used in two contexts and it is important that we understand each so that we don't become confused. The first refers to the state of Righteousness. The second refers to the fruit of Righteousness. Another way to put it is: The first is pertaining to what it takes to become righteous. The second pertains to what you will do now that you are righteous.

Let's take a look at what Jesus says about works as related to obtaining righteousness.

In the Gospel of John, chapter 6, Jesus is speaking to a crowd of people who had witnessed his feeding the multitudes with two fish and five loaves of bread. Jesus and His disciples, left the place where this miracle had occurred and crossed over the sea to Capernaum. When the people realized they had left, they went to Capernaum looking for Jesus. When they found him, they asked him a question which we see in John 6:28,29,

"Then they said to Him, "What shall we do, that we may work the works of God" 29 Jesus answered and said unto them, "This is the work of God, that you believe on Him who He sent".

These people were followers of Christ only in the sense that they had followed him across the sea to eat another fish buffet. They had not become Christ disciples at this point. Jesus answers them in a way to let them know that this encounter with Him had much more to do with their spiritual well-being, than with their physical hunger. In Verse 26, Jesus said to them, *"Most assuredly, I say to you, you seek Me, not because you saw the signs, but because you ate of the loaves and were filled. 27 Do not labor for the food which perishes, but for the food which endures to everlasting life, which the Son of man will give you, because God the Father has set His seal on Him."*

Jesus goes on to say in verse 35, *"I am the bread of life. He who comes to Me shall never hunger, and he who believes in me shall never thirst.*

Jesus told them, the only work you can do in order to receive eternal life is the work of believing on Him whom God has sent and He shall give you that eternal life. Righteousness is a free gift that comes with eternal life. Then later in John 14:12 Jesus speaking of the fruit of Righteousness says, He that believeth on me, the works that I do he will do also and greater works than these shall I do for I go to my Father.

Why did God make us righteous? Why is it important to be Righteousness conscious?

Our Father is a God of purpose. He has a plan for every one of us. He has chosen us for the purpose, noted in the John's gospel chapter 15:6, *"You have not chosen me, but I have chosen you, and ordained you, that ye should go and bring forth fruit and that your fruit should remain: that whatsoever you shall ask of the Father in my name, he may give it to you.* God desires for us to become fruit bearers. His commitment to us is to give us to everything we ask Him in Jesus's name in order to bear fruit.

All fruit starts out with a seed which must be planted. God desires that all of mankind be saved! The Word of God is a seed and He needs labourers, people who will sow it. Without the sowing or preaching (pro-claiming) of His Word, salvation will not come to those who are lost.

Even though Jesus died for the sins of the world, and though God is not willing that any should perish, salva-tion does not come automatically upon everyone who is lost. Only those who call upon the name of the Lord believing upon Him, will be saved. People will not call upon Him without believing he desires to save them. They will not believe without hearing the gospel. The gospel will not be heard until it is preached. Preaching the gospel of Jesus Christ is simply witnessing to others what Jesus has done for mankind in His death, burial and resurrection and ascension and seating at the right hand of God, out of His and the Fathers love for us.

Romans 10:8-15 New International Version (NIV)

8 But what does it (the scripture) say? "The word is near you; it is in your mouth and in your heart,"that is, the message concerning faith that we proclaim: 9 If you declare with your mouth, "Jesus is Lord," and believe in your heart that God raised him from the dead, you will be saved. 10 For it is with your heart that you believe and are justified, and it is with your mouth that you profess your faith and are saved.11 As Scripture says, "Anyone who believes in him will never be put to shame."2 For there is no difference between Jew and Gentile—the same Lord is Lord of alland richly blesses all who call on him, 13 for, "Everyone who calls on the name of the Lord will be saved."

14 *How, then, can they call on the one they have not believed in? And how can they believe in the one of whom they have not heard? And how* *can they hear without someone preaching to them? 15 And how can anyone preach unless they are sent? As it is written: "How beautiful are the feet of those who bring good news!"*

Matthew 24:14 - *And this gospel of the kingdom will be preached in all the world as a witness to all the nations, and then the end will come.*

Matthew 4:23 - *Jesus went throughout all Galilee, teaching in their synagogues, preaching the gospel of the kingdom, and healing all kinds of sickness and all sorts of diseases among the people.*

Mat 9:35 - *And Jesus went about all the cities and villages, teaching in their synagogues, preaching the gospel of the kingdom, and healing every sickness and every disease among the people.*

Mark 1:14-15 - *Now after John was put in prison Jesus came to Galilee, preaching the gospel of the kingdom of God is at hand. Repent and believe the gospel.*

Luke 4:43 - *Jesus said to them, I must preach the kingdom of God to the other cities also, because for this purpose I have been sent*

Luke 8:1 *Now it came to pass, afterward, that Jesus went through every city and village, preaching an bringing the glad tidings (the gospel) of the kingdom of God.*

Luke 16:16-17 - *The law and the prophets were until John. Since that time the kingdom of God has been preached, and everyone is pressing into it. And it is easier for heaven and earth to pass away than for one tittle of the law to fail.*

Luke 17:20,21 - *The kingdom of God comes without observation, it is within you* John 3:3 - *Except a man be born again, he cannot see the kingdom of God*

Acts 8:5 - *But when they believed Philip preaching the things concerning the kingdom of God and the name of Jesus Christ, they were baptized, both men and women.*

1 Corinthians 15:3-4 New International Version (NIV)3 For what I received I passed on to you as of first importance that Christ died for our sins according to the Scriptures, 4 that he was buried, that he was raised on the third day according to the Scriptures.

Chapter 11

———◆———

Gods Righteousness vs. Mans Righteousness

When we don't understand God's righteousness, we go about attempting to establish our own righteousness or right standing with God. Basically every religion is built upon attempting to do something, to earn or make oneself worthy of right standing with God. For the Jews who were given the law of Moses to live by, observing the law is the only way one can be right with God. The problem with the law is that man has never been, nor ever would be able to keep all the law. If you couldn't keep it all, then you kept none of it. God's purpose for the law was to prove to man that he is unable to do enough to make himself right with God, and to lead him to Christ who is the end of, or the fulfillment of, the law to everyone that believes. Believing on Jesus Christ, is the only way one can be made right with God. Jesus said, I am the Way, the Truth and the Life, NO MAN cometh to the Father but by me! Jesus is the Way to the Father, the Truth in whom we must believe and the Life that we receive when we believe on Him.

Paul writes in Romans 10:1-10 *Brothers my heart's desire and prayer to God for Israel is that they might be saved. 2 For I testify about them that they have a zeal for God, but not according to knowledge. 3 For, being ignorant of God's righteousness and seeking to establish their own righteousness, they did not submit to the righteousness of God. 4 Christ is the end of the law unto righteousness for everyone who believes. 5 For Moses writes about the righteousness which is based on the law; "The man who does those things shall live by them. 6 But the righteousness which is based on faith says, "Do not say in your heart "Who will ascend into heaven?" That is to bring Christ down), 7 or, "Who will descend into the deep? (that is to bring Christ up from the dead). 8 What does it (the scripture) say? "The word is near you, in your mouth and in your heart. This is the word of faith that we preach: that if you con-fess with your mouth Jesus is Lord, and believe in your heart that God has raised Him from the dead, you will be saved, 10 for with the heart, one believes unto righteousness and with the mouth confession is made unto salvation. 11 For the Scripture says, "Whosoever believes in Him will not be ashamed.*

In the beginning of this book, I shared the fact that I was inspired to write it as a result of a conversation I'd had with a close friend. During that conversation, which we were having over the phone as I was driving to work, he suggested that God was good to me, and that God was working on my behalf, because I had done something to deserve it.

Because I didn't want to be distracted while talking to him, I pulled onto a nearby parking lot so that I could give myself wholly to this vital matter. After spending a great deal of time explaining to him that we can do nothing to earn God's grace, mercy, love, salvation, or righteousness (right standing with Him), because it is a free gift, I felt it was necessary to invite him to accept God's gift at that moment. I explained to him that he could receive God's gift of salvation with which comes all of the wonderful provisions God has made available to us and asked if he'd like to pray at that moment to receive. I remember the excitement of my heart as I paused to hear his response. I was fully convinced he would say yes. After a short pause, he responded, "I'm not quite ready yet. There are some things I need to get right in my life first." It hit me like a ton of bricks and for a moment, I felt like I had utterly failed in my attempt to effectively communicate the gospel. I was so disappointed!

Once I regained my composure, I explained to him that we can never clean up our lives on our own. God does not expect us to. He accepts us just the way we are when we come to Him. After He comes into our hearts, He starts to reveal His nature and character to us through His Word and in the process of time, we start to see change in our lives. The Apostle Paul writes in the scripture above in Romans 10:3, that when we do not understand God's righteousness we go about attempting to establish our own righteousness (through our good works) failing to submit to the righteousness of God which we receive by faith. Well, the scriptures also tell us that at best our own righteousness is as filthy rags, that there is none righteous, no, not one as far as man's righteousness goes. Ephesians 2:8,9 says, For by grace are you saved through faith and that not of yourselves, it is a gift of God, not of works, lest any man should boast.

I wish I could tell you my friend said yes to my invitation to receive Jesus' gift that day, but I can't. I am encouraged however, that the seed of God's Word was sown into his heart and I believe that because of the faithfulness of God, somebody has watered it and that God will give it increase.

In order to obtain the Righteousness of God, faith is a must; We must believe it by faith, We must confess it by faith, We must receive it in faith! Faith in what? Faith in God's Word! Faith in God's promise!

Jesus has paid the price for our Righteousness once and for all! There is no excuse for anyone who has heard the Gospel of Jesus Christ and accepted it as truth, not to enjoy a life of righteousness for when we received Jesus Christ, He became our Righteousness and we were made the righteousness of God IN HIM. We are not waiting on Jesus to come down from heaven again or to come up from the grave again to do what he has already done. He'll never go to the grave again for our sins, and He'll never come down from heaven again to die on the cross, He has already done it and IT IS FINISHED!

So You might ask, "**How do I receive His Righteousness?** The Apostle Paul answers by asking this question. "What does the scriptures say? (The answer to all of life's questions is always in the scriptures). Paul goes on to answer this question; "this is what the scripture says," "the word is **near you**, it **is in your mout**h and **in your heart,** this is the word of faith which we preach...

How do I apply it? ...that if you confess with your mouth the Lord Jesus (or Jesus is Lord), and believe in your heart that God has raised Him from the dead, you will be saved...

How does this"faith" work? ...for with the **heart** man **believes unto righteousness** and with his **mouth, confession is made unto salvation!**

Won't you receive HIs Righteousness TODAY?

It is my desire that the Lord has spoken to your heart in and through this book! God wants to move all of us into his prefect and divine will. His desire is that we come to Him; come to know Him; come to grow In Him; become one with Him; and that we lead others to do the same! This journey begins with first inviting Jesus into your heart as Savior and Lord of your life.

If you have not already invited Him into your life, please pray this simple prayer:

Heavenly Father, I realize I am a sinner and I need You in my life. I come to You now repenting of my sins and asking You to forgive me of them all. I believe in my heart that You sent your Son Jesus Christ to die on the cross for all the sins of the world including my sins and that only His precious blood could wash them clean. I believe that You raised Jesus up from the dead on the third day, and now I ask You Jesus to come into my heart and I confess You now as my personal Savior and Lord. Amen

If you are already saved but your life as a Christian is powerless, empty or lacking vitality or fulfillment, please pray this simple prayer:

Heavenly Father, Jesus told his disciples that they would receive power after that the Holy Ghost had come upon them so that they would be witnesses of Him. After they received the baptism of the Holy Ghost, the evidence was that they became powerful witnesses as You worked with them by Your Holy Spirit con-firming your word with signs following. They prayed for the sick and the sick recovered, they spake with new tongues and ministered to the people with miracles and wonders wrought by the Holy Ghost. Father, I need the power of the Holy Ghost in my life. You said in Your Word that You would give the Holy Ghost to those who ask. I'm asking you now to baptize me with the Holy Ghost and with fire so that I can do the work you've called me to do! I receive it (the baptism in the Holy Ghost) by faith now, In Jesus Name !

If you are already saved and filled with the Holy Spirit, but you are struggling with knowing Gods will for your life, you may pray the prayers found in the Epistles or

letters written by the Apostle Paul to the believers in the 1st century churches. These prayers were penned by Paul, but inspired by the Holy Spirit. They can be found in the following scriptures: Ephesians 1 16-20

Ephesians 3:14-20 Phil. 1:9,10 Colossians 1:9-11

Heavenly Father, I ask you to give unto me the spirit of wisdom and revelation in the knowledge of Jesus Christ. I ask that You enlighten the eyes of my understanding that I may know what is the hope of His calling, and what is the riches of the glory of His inheritance in the saints and what is the exceeding greatness of His power towards us who believe. For this cause I bow my knees unto the Father of our Lord Jesus Christ from whom the whole family in heaven and earth is named, that You would grant me according to the riches of your glory to be strengthened with might by Your Spirit in the inner man, that Christ may dwell in my heart by faith, that I, being rooted and grounded in love, may be able to comprehend with all the saints, what is the breadth and length and depth and height and to know the love of Christ which passes knowledge; that I may be fill with all the fullness of God. I pray that my love may abound still more and more in knowledge and all discernment, that I may approve the things that are excellent, and that I may be sincere and without offense till the day of Christ, being filled with the fruits of righteousness which are by Jesus Christ, to Your glory and praise. Father I pray and ask that I may be filled with the knowledge of Your will in all wisdom and spiritual understanding; that I may walk worthy of the Lord, fully pleasing Him, being fruitful in every good work and increasing in the knowledge of God; strengthened with all might, according to His glorious power, for all patience and long suffering with joy. I thank you Father in the Name of Jesus, Amen.

About the Author

Tommie Brown is passionate about teaching God's Word. His passion has led him to teach in Churches and Bible Schools in North America, South America, Asia, Africa and Europe. Having witnessed the impact of the Gospel in his own life, he clearly understands Jesus' Commission to go into all the world and make disciples. Tommie is a 2003 graduate of Rhema Bible College in Tulsa, Oklahoma. He has served in various capacities of ministry for more than thirty years

CPSIA information can be obtained
at www.ICGtesting.com
Printed in the USA
LVHW041149290920
667372LV00003B/372